Lem

Endogo book 5

Published by Crossbridge Books
Worcester
© Crossbridge Books 2025

ISBN 978-1-916945-14-2

British Library Cataloguing Publication Data. A catalogue record for this book is available from the British Library.

CROSSBRIDGE
BOOKS

Lem

Endogo book 5

by R M Price-Mohr

Vocabulary for book 5:

be
big
fast
first
frame
get
had
having
him
it/It
made
next
play
race
tall
there
up
very
was
who/Who

Foreword for teachers

These books have been developed for older beginner readers. The research-based approach focuses on the recognition of just 100 key words that together make up approximately two-thirds of all reading matter in English.

For each new book, twenty new words are introduced and listed at the beginning of each book The new vocabulary for each book should be introduced to the learner in such a way that they will be able to recognise them at sight <u>before</u> reading the book. It is recommended that this is achieved through playing with the printed words. In the first instance, this should be by having two sets of printed and separated words in large font (minimum 20 point) that the beginner reader can match. It is crucial that the teacher continuously verbalise the words, and they may point to significant features in words, firstly the initial letters and secondly to any other distinctive features, to assist with the matching. Following this, the word recognition can be reinforced in games such as bingo, dominoes, snap, Pelmanism etc.

It is crucial that the teacher continue to verbalise the words during all the games, and the teacher should draw attention to the first letter of words and sound out that initial letter for the beginner.

Some temptations to avoid:

- Do not ask the reader to sound out all the individual letters of a word – only the initial letter has value at this stage for reading.
- Do not test the reader to see if they can recognise any of the words by telling you what they say – this should become obvious during the games; remember that visual recognition is not the same thing as verbalising what is seen.

This is Lem the endogo.

The lemur wants to play with him.

Lem had made a climbing frame.
It was very tall.

But the lemur was too big.

He will break it.

Pam wants to go up the climbing frame too.

The lemur is going to go up the tree next to the climbing frame.

They are having a race.

Who will be first?

Lem and Pam are very fast.

Suddenly, there is a very big and hungry bird.

Lem and Pam have to get away fast.

They run into the cave.

High Frequency Words:

be
big
fast
first
get
go
had
him
it
made
play
there
up
very
was
who

Word Patterns:

_all		_st	
	tall		fast
	all		first
	fall		forest
	small		
_y	hungry	_ing	looking
	happy		eating
	very		going
	suddenly		climbing
			having